RAMBLINGS FROM THE TRAIL

Wisdom Editions
Minneapolis

FIRST CALUMET EDITION JUNE 2023
Ramblings from the Trail: Wet Feet, Soiled Dress,
and Defining Historical Truth.
Copyright © 2023 by Vicki Pellar Price. All rights reserved.

10 9 8 7 6 5 4 3 2 1
ISBN: 978-1-960250-89-6

Cover and interior design: Gary Lindberg
Cover photo by Vicki Pellar Price

RAMBLINGS FROM THE TRAIL

Wet Feet, Soiled Dress, and Defining Historical Truth

Vicki Pellar Price

Wisdom
Editions
Minneapolis

Table of Contents

Introduction

Elizabeth Fries Ellet's name was circulating in Eden Prairie in the early 2000s. I had a lot of questions. Who was she? Why did she come to Minnesota? Why would a woman travel on her own in the 1850s? Maybe I was more curious than others because I had recently relocated to Minnesota in 1991 to fulfill a family dream. After I read about her, I discovered how maligned she had been–and still is–and that she was fulfilling her desire to establish herself as a writer whose literary reach went beyond most women of her era.

Compelled by what I uncovered through my research of this 19th-century writer and her travelogue of Minnesota, I approached the City of Eden Prairie— well known for its Historical Society, Plant a Tree Program, conservation of natural habitat and its thirty-seven parks—about creating an Elizabeth Fries Ellet storybook garden. I presented the concept to the Eden Prairie Heritage Foundation to locate it at Purgatory Creek Park. A final decision was made with the Eden Prairie Parks Department, approved by Mayor Nancy Tyra-Lukens and Eden Prairie Council members, who settled on the Richard T. Anderson Conservation Area and supported obtaining corporate sponsors for an interpretive trail, a plan confirmed and ratified in 2003.

What followed involved four years working on prototypes on my basement floor, taping images on huge sheets of butcher block paper; collecting scads of information gleaned from hundreds of sources, research and contacts with universities, libraries, botanists, birders and specialists; hiring a design firm and sign manufacturer; and seeking approvals from the City of Eden Prairie to make seven Interpretive signs at the Richard T. Anderson Conservation Area.

Maybe, in retrospect, this wasn't only about vindicating Ellet's reputation–and I will–it was about me too, my interest in the natural environment, especially after knowing she referred to this area as the "garden spot of the territory" in her travelogue and memoir *Summer Rambles in the West*. I too reestablished myself in a new place, but I found myself immersed in a city that I could become a part of, not only as a resident, but as a contributor.

This trail guide is part of my intention to return Ellet to the rank of creatives including George Catlin, Henry David Thoreau, and others who are credited with creating art and literature focused on uniquely American nationhood, national culture, and a sense of place apart from British Victorian writers.

One of my first immersive experiences with Ellet took place when I read *Summer Rambles in the West*. Part travelogue and memoir, the volume reveals her experiences far beyond her mid-1800s New York domicile. She is among the first white women to set foot—literally and figuratively—into the domain of men. I followed Ellet into her world where she described a lake near the Minnesota River as "a palette of gems," compared "(s)trawberry leaves with the brilliant red of Sumach (sic)," a landscape that "painters have failed to imitate."

Elizabeth Fries Ellet Interpretive Trail

http://www.efeinterpretivetrail.org
https://writersrisingup.org/

Seven signs in the nearly mile-long trail in the Richard T. Anderson Conservation Area in Eden Prairie offer only a hint of what it felt like for the 19th-century observer and writer for whom the trail is named. With this guide, you will be able to follow in her footsteps. She wrote about "setting aside the roughness of the way, treading ground," and you too can walk with her along the Elizabeth Fries Ellet Interpretive Trail (EFEIT), which has been an outdoor science and history lab since 2007.

Ellet was cognizant that the ground she walked on, ground she said white men had never reached, had been inhabited by people for over 12,000 years "from a period beyond the memory of tradition." Ellet understood the interaction between place as home, place as representing its people and place as an untouched natural environment for thousands of years, in what was becoming a region undergoing significant changes.

Ellet climbed the bluff line, taking in the prairie spread before her, and wrote in her travelogue-part-memoir *Summer Rambles in the West* that this may have been how the Garden of Eden looked. When she visited the Minnesota River Valley in the mid-1800s, Eden Prairie wasn't platted until 1853 and Shakopee would not be platted until 1854, after her excursion to Minnesota.

When nineteenth century American writers, naturalists, painters, illustrators, and photographers visited the "new territories" of the Midwest, they were taken with the natural spaces. Today, as walkers, observers, gardeners, naturalists, and storytellers, we demand more natural spaces and less concrete. We have a new understanding of the dynamic relationship between the air, the land, and the water upon which all life depends.

The history presented by the Elizabeth Fries Ellet interpretive signs on a path adjacent to the Minnesota River is a preview. Within these pages, you will witness her encounters with the flora and fauna of the region, the people who explored it, the pioneers who settled there, the Natives who lost their land, their way of life, the artisans and writers who captured it in their work.

Ellet's travelogue memoir is one of the first written in the nineteenth century by a woman. The experiences described include one in the vicinity of Little Falls Creek by the Mississippi River when her party came upon a "haystack," which was referred to as a "settlement." It was a sign of habitation that appeared suddenly in the midst of streams that led to the Minnehaha falls, forests, and a broad meadow.

Ellet camped out in the woods, slept under a tent, and was bitten by mosquitoes on trips that other ladies refused to go on. She was the only woman among a group of men on one journey to locate a new lake. She may have brought along boots and wood-soled shoes, which would have protected her from mud, rain, and terrain incompatible with regular shoes. She would have hiked the hills or boarded flatboats in practical skirts made of cotton and linen for the discovery of the new territory. Nothing deterred Ellet, and she would go wherever the men went. It seems unlikely she would have dressed like the ladies who only frequented the salons wearing hoop skirts, and breast-flattening corsets.

It was the heyday of steamboats when Ellet took the Ben Campbell in 1852, navigating Minnesota's rivers, and there were times she journeyed in smaller flatboats or keelboats, a horse-drawn carriage, a horse, or on "Customary Excursions" in which she secured a place in one of Willoughby and Power's stages for what was called the "grand tour" from St. Anthony Falls to Lake Harriet and Mde Maka Ska (aka Calhoun), Minnehaha Falls, Fort Snelling, and Spring Cave.

Eventually, Ellet's group rode a wagon to a lodge where they would rest from their journey. Some in the group left their luggage in the wagon and took a footpath to a boat to fish. They came upon a "bright sheet" of water, an arm of Lake Minnetonka. Ellet wrote, "as the first white women, whoever looked on its beauty, to bestow a name, in compliment to the English portion of our party we called it Lake Browning...after that great poetess."

Her determination to immerse herself in this landscape meant Ellet camped out in the wilds, infested with mosquitoes which necessitated a "smudge," a "short-lived primitive solution to stave off biting insects when there's not enough wood to burn." Ellet could ride for hours along rough roads in a carriage and hike in wet feet along muddy trails, and then write her way into history.

She could do what the men could do and, even more, insisted upon it. When the "ladies" in the group sat down in a shaded area with a view, a fellow male traveler said they were "out-of-bounds" and directed them to an area with a microscopic view. Ellet found these "masculine prejudices" unacceptable. Ultimately, the steamboat's captain provided seats to be placed in a section of the craft that provided a better view.

Unlike most of the women, dressed in what Ellet described as "ball-room" attire of laces, short sleeves, delicate fabrics, and low necklines, and who were often confined to their cabins, Ellet wore "weather-defying ginghams," "delaines," and worsted wool better suited to the weather and terrain.

Ellet's ruminations on how the Native American's lifestyle, once self-dependent, was now affected by annual payments from their white invaders, making them more dependent and drawn to interacting with traders of all kinds, selling novelties at expensive prices, was concerning to her.

Ellet wrote that she saw the Native Americans as primitive and uncivilized, compared to the burgeoning industrial society in which she lived. Observing Native Americans in transition was unavoidable and she identified what she saw as the disparity between "civilized life" and what she referred to as their "savage" lifestyle. Ellet believed industry, farming, and an improved culture of learning were "remedies" to making them more productive.

Even as their land was taken and lodges disappeared, she arrived during a time when she could still see them. Ellet wrote they were in "canoes or sitting in the parlors of hotels—the women in elaborate dress, painted, adorned with feathers, shells, bells, and perfume bottles or the warriors in bearskins and neckpieces of bear claws. Women carried papooses on their backs and would roam the streets to trade or beg and then return to distant encampments."

Ellet understood that in this landscape of the "glossy hue of the oak...a primeval forest, that Indians had held sway from a period beyond the memory of tradition." Some of Ellet's views in contrast to George Catlin, who wrote in his *Letters and Notes on the Manners, Customs, and Condition of the North American Indians*, published in 1841, "The world knows generally that they are mostly uncivilized, and consequently unchristianized... they are nevertheless human beings, with features, thoughts, reason, and sympathies like our own; but few yet know how they live, how they dress, how they worship, what are their actions, their customs, their religions, their amusements, etc., as they practice them in the uncivilized regions of their uninvaded country, which is the main object of this work." (vol. 1, p. 5). Catlin's fascination with Native Americans was piqued with the westward expedition of Meriwether Lewis and William Clark in the early 1800s. From 1830 to 1838 Catlin created images of Native people and their ways of life in paintings, prints, and writings. He arrived in Minnesota with his wife on the steamboat Warrior in 1835. The Catlins stayed at the Fort Snelling Agency, with Mrs. Catlin departing for St Louis in July to have a baby. Catlin took off in a bark canoe to Prairie du Chien, with documents from Lawrence Taliaferro, a U.S. Army officer at Fort Snelling and Indian agent, showing his support for Catlin's artistic skills and desire to paint images of Native Americans. Catlin's interest in capturing the images of every tribe resulted in travel by steamboat, horseback, and canoe, eventually contacting General William Clark to assist him in meeting with other Native American tribes. Catlin and Thoreau were linked by a shared fascination with the Native American life of the region.

Like Thoreau, Ellet not only championed the stewardship of the natural wonders she encountered, but the walking text, and historical writing. Thoreau wrote this about visiting Baker Farm, a short distance south of Walden pond: "sometimes I rambled to pine groves, standing like temples..." Ellet's travelogue about her time spent along the Minnesota shares a great deal with Thoreau's sojourns in the wild. Thoreau made the trip to Minnesota with Horace Mann, Jr., a botanist and the son of the nation's educational reformer. Although Mann made the trip in the hopes it would cure Thoreau's tuberculosis, Thoreau's real main interest was in plant observation and sampling. He made notes of what he saw, describing what has been referred to as the "Ecological Identity" of a community. His notes were published twice, but what he wrote has not been considered for inclusion in Minnesota's developing "literature of place," even though he writes about his trip along the Minnesota

River during which he traveled past an area that became Eden Prairie on his way to the Redwood Agency, where payment of annuities to the Sioux took place. Aside from this excursion, Thoreau showed an interest in Native Americans, their culture, and history. A writer for the *Minneapolis State Atlas* wrote about the distinguished guests aboard the Franklin Steele: Governor and Mrs. Mann, Horace Mann Jr., and Henry David Thoreau, who was referred to as an "Abolitionist." It was the only mention of Thoreau's trip by a Minnesota newspaper, maybe because Thoreau's notes contained his sense that the Native Americans were being robbed. Thoreau died in May 1862, nine months after his journey to Minnesota and just months before the bloody conflict between the Dakota and the U.S. Army.

Just as Ellet was likely the earliest white, female chronicler of the region, Emily Hitchcock Terry was its first white, female illustrator of the region. Terry came to Minnesota with her reverend husband and baby son on a train from Massachusetts. Her son died during the trip to Minnesota and her husband later succumbed to tuberculosis in Minnesota at the age of 36. Terry lived in Minnesota from 1872 to 1884 and was Minnesota's first botanical artist, working on 49 images of Minnesota flora and 61 species of Minnesota plants. It wasn't until 1913 that she presented a bound album which included

142 watercolors, A *Painted Herbarium*, to Smith College, her alma mater.

While Ellet's career followed a path of notoriety and profit, Terry's occupation was one of a solitary existence. Terry's work remained unknown for 100 years, but is work too valuable not to be noticed. In 1995 the governor of Minnesota proclaimed April 7 "Emily Hitchcock Terry Day," honoring Terry's contribution of the first plant distribution record for the state of Minnesota through her collections and paintings.

Another contemporary of Ellet who chronicled the region did not use paint or words, but the technologically advancing medium of photography. Joel Emmons Whitney arrived in Minnesota in 1860 and knew very little about photography until he met Alexander Hesler. Whitney's Gallery was above Charles D. Elfelt's store on Third Street and Cedar Avenue in St. Paul. He also produced the first daguerreotype of St Anthony Falls, which was seen by George Sumner at Hesler's Chicago studio and purchased in 1854 as a gift for his brother, Senator Charles Sumner of Massachusetts. The senator then presented it to his friend Henry Wadsworth Longfellow, who used it as inspiration for his famous poem, "Song of the Hiawatha."

In those days, photographers seldom signed their pictures, but Hesler did keep an account of where Whitney and he traveled in Minnesota to take pictures, so we have an idea of the pictures they took. Just imagine the equipment they had to carry through rough terrain. The process of creating a daguerreotype image involved plates of silver copper; polishing aids; buffers with chemicals like iodine, bromide, and chloride; toxins like mercury and sodium thiosulphate, Mercury use risked "mad-hatter syndrome," or mercury poisoning. In 1860, a safer glass negative process was adopted that could produce unlimited images.

The Mdewakanton Dakota Sioux leader Wabaṡa (also known as Wabasha, Wapasha, or Tahtapesaah), resided on the Lower Reservation established by the Indian Agency. He succeeded his father as head of their band of Dakota in 1836. He was also called Norman Wabasha. During the U.S.-Dakota War, the Dakota people were divided about fighting against the white man. Wabaṡa joined a group of Dakota called the Peace Party interested in ensuring the Dakotas' safety. After the war, Wabaṡa was exiled to Crow Creek, South Dakota, and later to Santee, Nebraska. Wabaṡa died on April 23, 1876, at the Santee Agency.

Wabaṡa wrote of his people's displacement, "We think our Great Father may have forgotten his Red children & our hearts are very heavy–the Agents he sends to us seem to forget their father's words before they reach here for we often think they disobey what he has said. . . . You have said you are sorry to see my young men engaged still in their foolish dances–it is because their hearts are sick. They don't know whether these lands are to be their home or not," wrote Wabasa (sic) to Bishop Whipple in 1862.

A set of signs along a trail is a deceptively simple presentation of a complex history of a region. In exploring Ellet's connection to the region, unexpected connections and relationships among and between the artists, writers, and leaders of the time were revealed, along with their complexities. As we work toward a world where historical truth is deepened and embraced, leading to a culture where the narratives do not shy away from our failings in creating a space that embraces diversity, equity, and inclusion, these stories illuminate the context of the time and offer a basis for conversations around these issues.

Ellet, Catlin, Thoreau, Terry, Cooper, Whitney, Wabaṡa –all are players in this drama as students of the human condition. It is essential that we come to better understand the dimensions of what inspired them, what drove them to explore this presumed "wilderness." At that time, the United States was in political, economic, and social turmoil. We are embroiled in the same struggles for understanding and agreement today.

With this guide, you can become an explorer of what life was like from the chronicled history and images from American artisans, writers, historians, and walkers of place in the 19th century. To create your own sense of place and connect with the people who were shaped by and who shaped this region—then and now. You can become a part of a shared legacy—Native Americans; European adventurers; first-, second-, and third-generation Americans—while understanding how a sense of place is indispensable to humans, because through that we are compelled to steward the natural world. As naturalists, walkers, birders, history buffs, and any who appreciate a good story, we are learning even more deeply the profound, prescient truth of Walt Whitman's words in "The Lesson of a Tree" when he wrote, "in wildness is the preservation of the world."

Chapter 1:
Ellet–Women's Historian, Prolific Writer, Feminist

As a girl, Ellet attended the Aurora Female Seminary in Aurora New York. Her upbringing was in the tradition of the nineteenth century role into which women of privilege were born—women should be educated so far as it supported their duties within the home: caring for children, running a household, and understanding their gender role in society.

Being a writer was not an acceptable role for women in that era, but Ellet followed the passions of women before her, who were adept at crafting words into images of nineteenth century life, who wrote anonymously under male pseudonyms in order to be accepted and then published posthumously. Ellet pursued her passion for writing and published her first book, *Poems*, in 1835 at the age of sixteen.

TRAIL GUIDE
ELIZABETH FRIES ELLET
INTERPRETIVE TRAIL

Library of Congress

LOCATED AT THE
RICHARD T. ANDERSON
CONSERVATION AREA

At seventeen Ellet married chemist Dr. Henry William Ellet, a graduate of Columbia College in New York in 1824. They moved to South Carolina where he was a professor of chemistry, mineralogy, and geology at South Carolina College in 1836. Dr. Ellet received a gold medal for a dissertation on the compounds of cyanogen and was awarded for his discovery of a new and inexpensive means of preparing guncotton. Despite his accomplishments, Ellet's husband remains but a footnote in her larger legacy as a prolific female writer, including her singular contribution to women's history, in an era when only male writers dominated that genre.

While living in South Carolina Ellet published in the *Southern Literary Journal and Monthly Magazine* and *Southern Literary Messenger*, though she still wrote for national magazines and newspapers.

In 1845, Ellet began traveling between South Carolina and New York. Dr. Ellet eventually moved back to New York permanently to become a consulting chemist at the Manhattan gas company and held that office until his death in 1859. Ellet's decision to move back to New York resulted from feeling detached from the literary opportunities which abounded in New York, and relationships with writers, poets, and members of the New York literary society and the press. Ellet's move back to her home state was her first foray into the literary world of esteemed American writers known worldwide. While emerging into the New York literary scene of soirees and social gatherings, Ellet was a free agent, a career woman, not a woman of domesticity as prescribed by the mores of acceptable 19th-century females.

Ellet was the first woman to write about women's historical roles in the American Revolution, in Elizabeth Fries Ellet's book, *The Women of the American the Revolution*, she wrote extensively, in three volumes, about women, whose strictly domestic roles changed, as they too became defenders of what was to become an independent nation. Throughout her book *Summer Rambles in the West*, she demonstrated that women did not have to be confined to only domestic roles. In one such occurrence in Minnesota when men set out to fish and hunt, they regarded a female going with them as an impossibility. Ellet's response was to question "why a woman couldn't keep her seat in a wagon as well as a man." Ellet considered it "masculine selfishness," in their refusal to allow women to share in the experience of this new place.

Ellet's independent nature led her not only in crossing the lines of male literary dominance, but her travels extended her literary reach to writing a travelogue from a woman's perspective.

Ellet camped out in the woods, slept under a tent, and was bitten by mosquitoes on trips that other ladies refused to go on. She was the only woman among a group of men on one journey to locate a new lake. It's likely that she may have brought along boots and wood-soled shoes, which would have protected her from mud, rain, and terrain incompatible with regular shoes. It's also likely that on occasion, she wound up with mud-soaked, wet feet.

She would have hiked the hills or boarded flatboats in practical skirts made of cotton and linen for discovery of the new territory. It seems unlikely she would have dressed like the ladies who only frequented the salons wearing hoop skirts and breast-flattening corsets. Nothing deterred Ellet, and she would go wherever the men went.

Chapter 2:
No Place for Ladies–The
Impracticality of a Carriage
When There Are No Roads

It was the heyday of steamboats when Ellet took the Ben Campbell in 1852. During her journey along Minnesota's rivers, she also traveled in smaller flatboats or keelboats, by horse-drawn carriage, and on horseback. As part of a "customary excursion," she secured a spot in one of Willoughby and Power's stagecoaches for what was called the "Grand Tour" from St. Anthony Falls to Lake Harriet and Bde Maka Ska, Minnehaha Falls, Fort Snelling, and Spring Cave.

On one excursion to an unnamed sheet of water, all agreed with Ellet's suggestion to name it Lake Bryant, after the poet by William Cullen Bryant. The group walked along a foot path through woods filled with deer and birds and inlets with water so clear they could see the sandy bottom and fish. Ellet said a landscape gardener would have approved. One gentleman with her group said he had stolen an egg out of an eagle's nest and was attacked by the mother eagle.

Ellet referred to a narrow isthmus of Lake Bryant as Point Wakon, an anglicized Dakota term for something of spiritual or of supernatural importance. She wrote about signs of Dakota worship, as the trees, ground and alters, still wore their presence.

On other excursions Ellet recounted men who were intent on fishing taking a footpath to a bend in a stream, eventually their party was seated in a boat, paddling up what Ellet described as "serpentine windings, banks fringed with willows and bushes, with here and there, a clump of trees, tastefully disposed…"

Animals surrounded them, including a pelican, a wild goose, and deer, and on another excursion, she described tree boughs and vines shading "wild plums, crab apples, grapes, and indigenous fruits, with strawberries, blackberries and cranberries in their season."

Ellet camped out in the woods, slept under a tent, and was bitten by mosquitoes on trips that other ladies refused to go on. She would not have hiked the hills or boarded flatboats in long bloomers, hoop skirts, or a breast-flattening corset. Nothing deterred Ellet, and she would go wherever the men went.

Ellet described how once, with a guide to show the way, the group took a path "so narrow as scarcely affording room for passage, the road disappearing through the trackless wild" and of descending a dangerous pitch in a double wagon that accommodated the group. On another outing Ellet learned some of her fellow female travelers were persuaded not to come by "croakers, who assured them Minnetonka was no place for ladies." In the nineteenth century, "croaker" meant a vocal pessimist, grumbler, or doomsayer. On an excursion when there were no roads, it was described by the men as "perfectly impossible" for women. Ellet's response was that it was "masculine selfishness, overbearing exclusiveness."

Chapter 3:
A Grass Couch for
Accommodations–Living Outdoors

Ellet's travelogue memoir *Summer Rambles in the West* is the first written in the 19th century by a woman. The experiences described include one in the vicinity of Little Falls Creek by the Mississippi River, when her party came upon a "haystack," which was referred to as a "settlement." It was a sign of habitation that appeared suddenly in the midst of streams that led to the Minnehaha falls, forests, and a broad meadow. Ellet referred to "hermits hay" made into a couch by a plainly-dressed farmer. Ellet called him a "recluse" and the sight of him was disappointing to her; she would have "preferred seeing a man in skins or even an Indian blanket," which attests to her unfamiliarity with the realities of the new west compared to New York. "Hermits hay" was a 17th,

19th century term for people who were hired to live as hermits in make believe, so-called hermitages constructed on the grounds of grand estates.

As it turned out, he was not a "hermit," at all, but a friend of a fellow traveler, Mr. S, who was readying the area for a house to be built. Despite its appearance, Ellet wrote Mr. S apologized for the accommodations, saying "he had wished they waited until it was a little nicer, a house built and so forth."

Ellet described the toilet as a tin washbasin with a looking glass and towels hanging near it. She wrote of a mosquito bar over a bed, which she described as a "shake -down of straw," a likely deterrence she had no use for in New York. Ellet described the lodge as "the most unpoetical place" she had ever been to.

Some in the group left their luggage in the wagon and took to a footpath to a boat to fish. They came upon a "bright sheet" of water, an arm of Lake Minnetonka. Ellet wrote, "as the first white women, whoever looked on its beauty, to bestow a name, in compliment to the English portion of our party we called it Lake Browning…after that great British poetess, Elizabeth Barrett Browning, who was a contemporary. In 1850, Browning's *Sonnets from the Portuguese*, written in secret before she was married, was dedicated to her husband.

Chapter 4:
A Leap of Faith from New York City–Witnessing Lives of Native Americans

In the company of other women, while collecting Cornelians on the Mississippi shoreline, Ellet spotted a Sioux woman roasting a heron. Ellet described the bird as long-legged, long-necked being sizzled over a hand-made fire. The onlookers watched as the Indians feasted on roasted claws and entrails, while the rest of the Heron stew was cooking.

Seeing this evoked Ellet's ruminations on their lifestyle, once self-dependent, they were now given annual payments which made them more dependent and drawn to interacting with traders of all kinds, selling worthless novelties at expensive prices. Ellet referred to most of the items being sold as "geegaws."

Their way-of-life was interrupted by the so-called "civilized" lifestyle of their intruders in Ellet's eyes. She saw them as primitive, uncivilized as compared to the burgeoning industrial society that she lived in.

Observing Native Americans in transition was unavoidable...the disparity between civilized life and what she referred to as their "savage" lifestyle. Ellet believed industry, farming, and an improved culture of learning were remedies to making them more productive.

As their land was taken and lodges disappeared, she could still see them in their canoes and sitting in the parlors of hotels in elaborate dress, painted, adorned with feathers, shells, bells, and perfume bottles or warriors in bear skins and neck pieces of bear claws.

Women carried papooses on their backs with not much else to do but roam the streets to trade, beg and then return to distant encampments. One Native woman who frequented the hotel, who was said to have a European-American lover, gave Ellet glass beads and another lady a pewter ring as tokens of remembrance.

On another excursion, the group Ellet was traveling with learned of an Oval Stone placed between sticks, with red paint and yellow spots found near a lake. Evidently, it was this same place Dakota Indians visited for generations. A Dakota Sioux chief told them it's where they ceremoniously placed scalps after returning from battle; the spots marking the number of braves who participated.

Civilization as Ellet knew it in New York was displaced by what she referred to as "exclamations of stained strawberry leaves and the more brilliant red of sumac, the somber yellow of the hazel and the fading green of Cornus tribes, mingling with the bright glossy hue of the oak.." (she spelled it sumach), a primeval forest," that Indians had held sway from a period beyond the memory of tradition."

Ellet was creating literature by walking and observing nature as Thoreau did, as an environmentalist and naturalist. Like her contemporary Thoreau, she observed and recorded the wilds of Minnesota. Despite Thoreau's reputation as "New England's Hermit" he traveled the nation, including thousands of miles at the end of his life to witness the new Minnesota Territory, while afoot, as much as he could considering his advanced tuberculosis. Walking was not a studied or popular sub-genre in American letters, and those who wrote about walking and their motivations for taking to foot are more diverse than perhaps expected.

"Beautiful Day. Pleasant Walk: Walking and Landscape in the Works of Estwick Evans, John. D. Godman, Elizabeth Fries Ellet, and Bradford Torrey" responded to the natural world as they created a literary genre not known to Americans. Walking, traveling, discovery is what inevitably led to building places, communities, and in these discoveries, walking became more than just a way to get around.

Chapter 5:
Men Who Would Become
Part of the Founding
History of Minnesota

On August 11 the participants on this trip to Minnetonka journeyed over unknown terrain in a double wagon equipped with food from the St. Charles House larder in St Paul, along with blankets, comforters, and luggage.

They crossed over to Nicollet Island and Bde Maka Ska (Lake Calhoun), then on to a stretch of untraveled dirt until they came upon water like a mirror reflecting the sun and a beach. Then an Indian trail, marsh and prairie and onto another lake called "The Lake of the Isle of Red Cedars," though Ellet wrote there were no cedars.

Ellet witnessed "(m)iles more through scrub oak, hazel, wild cherry bushes, then groves of Tamarac and meadows of marsh grass," on her journey to the lake. Ellet is described in Early American Nature Writers, A Biographical Encyclopedia, with others, including Ralph Waldo Emerson, Thomas Jefferson, Henry David Thoreau, James Fenimore Cooper, and George Catlin, as historical men and women who wrote about nature.

Ellet had a lifelong relationship with nature, which is reflected in her early poems and resurfaced in her book *Summer Rambles in the West*. Ellet brings the reader along on her journey with vivid descriptions, not just of flora and fauna, but places and people she met on the way, another first, one of the first American travelogues written by a woman.

Her wagon journey to the Big Water "passing beyond civilization" was not without its perils, the group loaded on a heavy wagon, horses slowly trudging the narrow path that descended on one side. Ellet had heard the lake was 25 to 40 miles in length. The Native Indians referred to the lake as "Big Water," naming it Minne-tonka or Mide-tonka. Ellet wrote that the first name was readily accepted by all.

Ellet wrote, "When it was noised about that a new lake, of surprising magnitude had been found, a group of visitors including Colonel J.H. Stevens, one of the first residents of the area that's now Minneapolis, and Mr. Franklin Steele and others set out to see the lake.

In truth the lake was first cited by two teen boys in 1922, but few Euro-Americans knew of its existence until three decades later. Lake Minnetonka was officially named by the state's territorial Governor, Alexander Ramsey, in 1852,

Ellet wrote that it was Steele and Franklin's initial citing of the new lake that created wide-spread interest. Steven and Franklin were friends who did business ventures together. Steele bought Fort Snelling, leasing it back to the government. After the Civil War, Steele leased the land to settlers in the new territory, to become a state in 1858. Steele's business sense and investments in lumber sales, a suspension bridge, and land deals created growth which he prospered from. Steele donated four acres to the newly-created University of Minnesota.

Ellet was attuned to these events and that these men would likely become a part of the founding history of Minnesota, as would she, in part for her summer travelog, *Summer Rambles in the West.*

Chapter 6:
Ellet's Travails of "Sallying Mosquitoes"

Ellet camped out in the wilds, infested with mosquitoes which necessitated a "smudge," a "short-lived primitive solution to stave off biting insects when there's not enough wood to burn." Imagine hiking the hills or boarding a flatboat in hoop skirts and breast-flattening corsets compared to today's dress standards. The fashion of Jenny Lind lace or crochet collars and full bishop sleeves were also popular then, along with print and checked fabrics, tiered cape-like jackets, and the fullest of skirts made of readily available cotton and linen. As stated earlier, Ellet likely did not wear hoops skirts and corsets on long excursions over muddy trails and camping out.

Ellet could ride for hours along rough roads in a carriage and hike in wet feet along muddy trails, and then write her way into history. She could do what the men could do and, even more, insisted upon it. It is described that, when on the steamboat Ben Campbell, en route to Minnesota, the ladies sat down in a shaded area with a view and were told they were "out-of-bounds," by a fellow male traveler and directed to an area with a microscopic view. These "masculine prejudices," as Ellet described them, were unacceptable. The captain happened by and arranged for seats to be placed in a section of the ship that provided an excellent view.

Chapter 7:
Thoreau on the Franklin Steele Steamer 300 Miles Up the Minnesota River

Henry David Thoreau made the trip to Minnesota with Horace Mann, Jr., a botanist and the son of the nation's educational reformer, in an attempt to cure his tuberculosis. Thoreau's main interest was in plant observation and sampling. He made notes of what he saw, describing what has been referred to as the "Ecological Identity" of a community. His notes were published twice, but what he wrote was not considered for inclusion in Minnesota's developing "literature of place."

Henry David Thoreau

Thoreau and Mann's long journey from Concord, Massachusetts finally ended in St Paul at two to three in the morning. At six in the morning, they went to the American Hotel for breakfast, which is still well preserved. Then they took a stage coach through a rainstorm and stopped at the Tremont House close to the Falls of St Anthony. They stayed at the house of a widow near the lake, swam and drank water right out of the lake.

Mann's notes were detailed as to where they visited, what sites they were able to visit, like Minnehaha Falls. They even went game hunting. Mann had his gun along and shot birds, chipmunks, gophers, grosbeaks and bought a five-gallon barrel and alcohol to store them in.

Thoreau and Mann boarded the Franklin Steele on their trip on the Minnesota River and traveled past an area that became Eden Prairie on his way to the Redwood Agency, where a payment of annuities to the Sioux took place. Aside from this excursion,

Thoreau had previously shown much interest in Native Americans, their culture, and history. The Pioneer and The Democrat papers in St. Paul published stories that several thousand Sioux would be attending the event in Redwood and the event was Thoreau's singular attendance related to the Native Americans.

The Franklin Steele and other steamboats took off for Redwood with The Great Western Band. A writer for the Minneapolis State Atlas wrote about the distinguished guests aboard the Franklin Steele: Governor and Mrs. Mann, Horace Mann Jr., and Henry David Thoreau, who was referred to by the paper as an Abolitionist. It was the only mention of Thoreau's trip by a Minnesota newspaper.

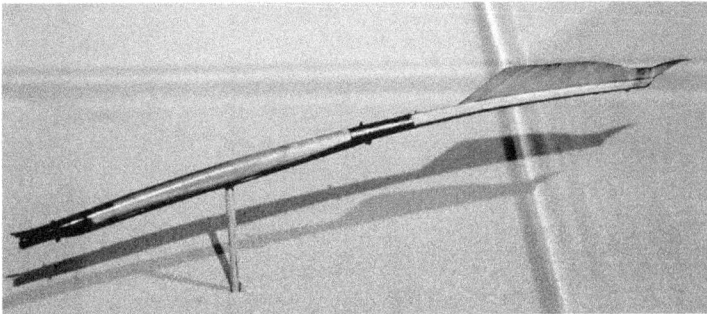

Thoreau's Writing Pen

About the trip, Thoreau wrote in a letter to his biographer Mr. Sanborn, "The Governor of Minnesota (Ramsey), the superintendent of the Indian Affairs in this quarter, and the newly appointed Indian agent were on board, also a German band from St. Paul, a small cannon for salutes, and the money for the Indians (aye and the gamblers, it was said, who were to bring it back in another boat.) There were about 100 passengers chiefly from St. Paul, and more or less recently from the N. Eastern states; also, half a dozen young educated Englishmen."

Thoreau's observations of the Indians at the Redwood Agency, written up in The Mankato Press, that "(t)hey were quite dissatisfied with the white man's treatment of them and probably have reason to be so... Speeches made on both sides ... Indians, as usual, having the advantage in truth and earnestness (over the white man)."

Thoreau died nine months after his journey to Minnesota. He passed away in May 1862, just months before the bloody conflict between the Dakota and the U.S. Army.

Chapter 8:
James Fenimore Cooper's
Leatherstocking Tales–
The American Frontier

James Fenimore Cooper was born in 1789 and raised in the forested village his father founded in Cooperstown, New York, the Great Northern Catskills. He was the first European-American to write about Native Americans in the *Leatherstocking Tales* series, a reflection of his frontier hometown. Cooper's series depicted the West as a work of myth and reality with fictional character Natty Bumppo as an American hero.

OUR CONTRIBUTORS.
Nº XII.

James Fenimore Cooper

Cooper gained most of his knowledge of Mohawk Indians from his stay in Cooperstown. Cooper had childhood knowledge of Native Indians. He was the first American to write about them. In his wife Susan's memoirs, she wrote that he talked with members of the Pawnee and Sioux nations.

Cooper deemed America's westward expansion a proper subject for literary works including The Pioneers published in (1823), *The Last of the Mohicans* (1826), *The Prairie* (1827), and *The Deerslayer* (1841), part of Cooper's Leather Stocking Tales.

Cooper was part of the Romantic Literary movement, from 1830 to 1870. The movement's focus was nature, symbolism, transcendentalism, and individualism. Authors like Emily Dickinson, Ralph Waldo Emerson, Harriet Beecher Stowe, and Walt Whitman, were some of its members. Edgar Allen Poe was considered a dark Romanticist.

There are stories in Sodus Bay that Cooper came to Charles Point in 1826 and occupied a shack on the point where residents said he accumulated an interest in local Native American tribes, according to Sodus Bay history. Cooper had two sisters who owned a cabin in Sodus Bay where Ellet was born sometime around 1818.

Cooper wrote about the American Revolution for his second book and composed the first important American historical novel, *The Spy* (1821). It received critical and financial success. In 1922 Cooper moved to New York City with his family to begin a career in writing. In 1851 Cooper died in Cooperstown, New York, his birthplace.

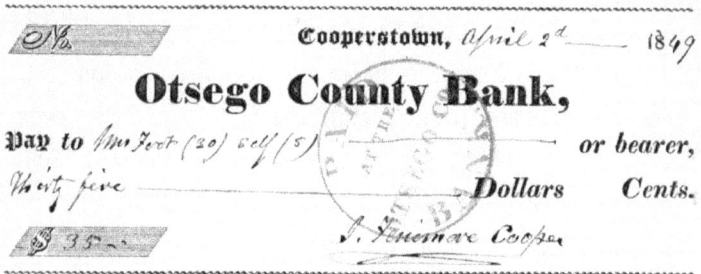

Check written by James Fenimore Cooper for thirty-five dollars from Otsego County Bank in Cooperstown, New York

It's no wonder that in July 1842, Ellet wrote to Mr. Cooper and asked for assistance in research she was doing for her book, *Women of the American Revolution*. Ellet wrote, "My book is in press and the printers proceed very rapidly; so that I am much hurried and full of anxiety for fear of mistakes. Scarcely any authorities agree with each other with regard to facts; and tradition I find cannot at all be depended on. I have received many interesting anecdotes which I am compelled to reject because they cannot be substantiated, and in some cases conflict with historical facts." Although Cooper traveled Europe and the United States eastern territories, he did not venture beyond the Albany-New York-Philadelphia-Baltimore-Washington corridor.

Chapter 9:Edgar Allen Poe–
Poet, Writer, Critic, Publisher

Edgar Allen Poe

Edgar Allen Poe was a participant in New York's Literary Soirees held at Anne C. Lynch Botta's at 116 Waverly Place in New York City. *The New Yorker* published an article in 1936 about her salon, referring to the gatherings as "an immense success, crowded weekly with famous writers, artists, journalists, and even actresses & actors."

With the publication of *The Raven* in the *New York Mirror*, Poe's popularity in the spring and early summer of 1845 resulted in his attendance at Lynch's literary soirees frequented by a "Blue Stocking" coterie of female writers of New York's Literary Society. "Blue Stocking" was a designation originally given to 18th century European female writers associated with feminist scholarship.

Poe became editor of the weekly *Broadway Journal*, published from 1845 to 1846 which contained Poe's writings and critiques of other writers. *Broadway Journal* was filled with the work of the Blue Stocking clique, its pages evolving into exchanges between Poe's many admirers competing for his attention and complimentary reviews.

Poe also worked for The Southern Literary Messenger, Burton's Gentleman's Magazine, American Monthly Magazine, American Museum of Science, Literature, and the Arts, and published in many others including Dollar Newspapers; Godey's Lady's Book; and the Broadway Journal, over which he had editorial control for a short time. Mr. Poe's movements through his life time, from birth to death began with his birth in Massachusetts, a childhood in East London, England, attendance at the University of Virginia, military service at Fort Moultrie in

South Carolina, he lived in three different homes in Pennsylvania, served at West Point in New York and he was laid to rest in Baltimore.

Bill for a Suit of Clothes

Made for Poe to wear home for the Christmas Holidays from the University of Virginia in December, 1826, rendered to JOHN ALLAN by SAMUEL LEITCH, Jr., apparently a Charlottesville tailor. POE was anxious to make a good appearance in the eyes of Miss ROYSTER, who, although he did not know it, was already engaged to another man through parental persuasion

From the Ellis & Allan files

Edgar Allen Poe Bill for Clothing

Chapter 10:
Chief Wabasa–
Mdewakanton Sioux

Chief Wabaśa (also known as Wabasha or Tahtapesaah), a member of the Mdewakanton band of Dakota, resided on the Lower Reservation by the Agency. He succeeded his father as head of their band of Dakota in 1836. He was also called Norman Wabasha. During the U.S.-Dakota War, the Dakota people were divided about fighting against the white man. Wabaśa joined a group of Dakota called the Peace Party interested in ensuring the Dakotas' safety. After the war, Wabaśa was exiled to Crow Creek, South Dakota, and later to Santee, Nebraska. Wabaśa died on April 23, 1876, at the Santee Agency.

"We think our Great Father may have forgotten his Red children & our hearts are very heavy—the Agents he sent to us seem to forget their father's words before they reach here for we often think they disobey what he has said. You have said you are sorry to see my young men engaged still in their foolish dances—it is because their hearts are sick. They don't know that whether these lands are to be their home or not," wrote Wabaśa to Bishop Whipple in 1862.

WHITNEY.   **OLD BETS.**   ST. PAUL.

A Sioux Squaw who will long be remembered with gratitude by many of the Minnesota Captives, for her kindness to them while among the Sioux in 1862.

Old Bets 1862. Joel Emmons Whitney daguerrotype.

In An Inventory of Bishop Henry B. Whipple Records at the Minnesota Historical Society, it states, "In the early years of his episcopate, Whipple's espousal of Indian reform and commitment to Indian missions earned him the enmity of many whites who hated Indians, and led some of his fellow bishops to look upon him as a fanatic. His attitude was denounced most bitterly after the U.S.-Dakota War of 1862, when, in appeals to the President and in the public press, he opposed wholesale executions and extermination or deportation of the Dakota."

Chapter 11:
Illustrator in the Wild–
Emily Hitchcock Terry

Emily Hitchcock Terry came to Minnesota with her husband Reverend Cassius Terry and a baby son on a train from Massachusetts. Her son died on the trip to Minnesota and her husband died of tuberculosis in Minnesota at the age of 36. She lived in Minnesota from 1872 to 1884 and was Minnesota's first botanical artist, working on 49 images of Minnesota Flora and 61 species of Minnesota plants. It wasn't until 1913 that she presented a bound album which included 142 watercolors, Painted Herbarium, to Smith College, her alma mater.

Emily Hitchcock Terry

The album was 18 1/2 inches high and 14 1/2 inches wide and four inches thick, including 61 species of plants. The species of plants and locations are identified, and the size of the paintings vary from five to over fifteen inches with widths from three to twelve inches.

On September 26, 1914, Emily wrote a letter to a friend and botanist, Walter Deane, seeking his opinion on her paintings of Minnesota flora that she had compiled in her Painted Herbarium, consisting of some paintings she had since she was a child.

While Ellet's career followed a path of notoriety and profit, Terry's occupation was one of a solitary existence. Terry's work remained unknown for 100 years, but her work was too valuable not to be noticed. In 1993, Minnesota artists who practiced a more modern version of capturing flora met. It was 100 years since Terry started painting Minnesota Flora, and it took three botanical artists to memorialize Terry in *Emily Hitchcock Terry 1838-1921, Minnesota's First Botanical Artist,* published by the American Society of Botanical Artists, researched and written by Wendy Brockman and Marilyn Garber.

Another book, *A Painted Herbarium: The Life and Art of Emily Hitchcock Terry (1838-1921)*, was written by Beatrice Scheer Smith and published by the University of Minnesota Press (1992). The book includes Terry's biography, many text illustrations, and forty-six full-color plates of her Minnesota-inspired paintings.

Finally in 1995 the governor of Minnesota proclaimed April 7 *Emily Hitchcock Terry Day.* Terry had created the first plant distribution record for the state of Minnesota through her collections and paintings.

Chapter 12:
George Catlin–Artist, Friend and Recorder of Native Americans in the 19th Century

George Catlin was born July 26, 1776, in Wilkes-Barre, Pennsylvania, and died December 23, 1872, in Jersey City, New Jersey. On November 3, 1776, John Adams defeated Thomas Jefferson, in the U.S. presidential election, our first President George Washington gave his farewell address. In a letter titled to *Friends and Citizens,* Washington warned forces of "geographical sectionalism, political factionalism, and interference" by foreign powers in the nation's domestic affairs threatened the stability of the republic. He urged Americans to subordinate sectional jealousies to common national interests.

George Catlin

As the story goes, when George Catlin was just a boy of nine in 1805, he came upon an Oneida Indian. Catlin was scared and the Oneida Indian extended his hand and friended Catlin, who had been exploring the Oneida woods, at that time more than six million acres from the St Lawrence River to the

Susquehanna River. It was the Oneida who became the first allies of the new pioneers fighting for their independence during the Revolutionary War. The meeting between Catlin and an Oneida had a lasting effect on the young Catlin.

George Catlin aptly assessed how Indians were considered by white men in his Letters and Notes on the Manners, Customs, and Conditions of the North American Indians, published in 1841, "The world knows generally that they are mostly uncivilized, and consequently un-christianized...they are nevertheless human beings, with features, thoughts, reason, and sympathies like our own; but few yet know how they live, how they dress, how they worship, what are their actions, their customs, their religions, their amusements, etc., as they practice them in the uncivilized regions of their uninvaded country, which is the main object of this work." (vol. 1, p. 5)

Catlin's fascination with Native Americans piqued with the westward expedition of Meriwether Lewis and William Clark in the early 1800s. From 1830 to 1838 Catlin created images of Native people and their ways of life in paintings, prints, and writings. He arrived in Minnesota with his wife on the steamboat Warrior in 1835. The Catlins stayed at the Fort Snelling Agency, with Mrs. Catlin departing for St Louis in July to have a baby. Catlin took off in a bark canoe to Prairie du Chien, with documents from

Lawrence Taliaferro, a U.S. Army Officer at Fort Snelling and Indian agent, showing his support for Catlin's artistic skills and desire to paint images of Native Americans. Catlin's interest in capturing the images of every tribe resulted in travel by steamboat, horseback, and canoe, eventually contacting General William Clark to assist him in meeting with other Native American tribes. At the time, Clark was the government's Superintendent of Indian Affairs for Western Tribes. Clark took Catlin to Fort Crawford, in Prairie du Chien, Wisconsin where the Sauk, Fox, and Sioux were having a council.

On one of Catlin's excursions, he convinced the Ojibwe and Iowa to reenact hunts, dances, even scalpings.

George Catlin Painting of Pipestone Quarry

Catlinite, a natural mudstone found in Pipestone, Minnesota, is named after George Catlin who visited the quarries in Minnesota in 1835. Catlin painted the pipestone quarry in 1836 and brought fame to the pipestone quarries with his artwork of Indians. Additionally, Catlin is said to have proposed the creation of a "nation's park" in the 1830s to preserve both the bison herds and Native cultures of the Great Plains. The notion was ignored for forty years.

Chapter 13:
Joel Emmons Whitney and His St. Paul Studio–The Daguerreotype

Whitney arrived in Minnesota with his father in 1850 and knew very little about photography until he met Alexander Hesler, who was a daguerreotypist with four years of experience. On an excursion in 1851, Hesler took his first daguerreotype images of St. Anthony Falls and Whitney became his student.

Joel Emmons Studio, Whitney's Gallery on 3rd Street in St Paul: Courtesy of A Writers Rising Up Projects Submission

Whitney's Gallery was above Charles D. Elfelt's store on Third Street and Cedar Avenue in St. Paul. His associate Alexander Hesler made the first daguerreotype of St Anthony Falls. One of Hesler's daguerreotype images was seen by George Sumner at Hesler's Chicago studio and Sumner purchased it in 1854 as a gift for his brother, Senator Charles Sumner of Massachusetts. The senator then presented it to his friend Henry Wadsworth Longfellow, who used it as inspiration for his famous poem, *Song of the Hiawatha*.

In those days, photographers seldom signed their pictures. The photographer was often undetermined. What's interesting is there is no evidence other than recollections written down by Hesler to indicate that the photos taken of Fort Snelling, the Falls of St Anthony and the Suspension Bridge across the Mississippi were in fact produced by Whitney and Hesler.

But Hesler did keep an account of where Whitney and he traveled in Minnesota to take pictures, so we only have an idea of the pictures they actually took. Hesler made many copies of his daguerreotypes, one was a portrait of Abraham Lincoln for his 1860 presidential campaign, which was printed in the thousands.

Just imagine the equipment they had to carry through rough terrain. The process of creating a daguerreotype image involved plates of silver copper; polishing aids; buffers with chemicals like iodine, bromide, and chloride; and mercury, a toxic substance; and sodium thiosulphate, a non-toxic substance, all employed in the process of exposing the image. Mercury use risked "mad-hatter syndrome," or mercury poisoning. The daguerreotype process was toxic and arduous and was ultimately replaced in 1860 with a safer glass negative process that could produce unlimited images.

Chapter 14:
Projects—Ways to Experience
the Mid-1800s at Any Age

Areas of research and opportunities to make class presentations, scrapbooks of plant cuttings, cut-out dolls of what women wore in the 1850s, preparing a Sioux meal, growing a pioneer kitchen garden, class nature walks, experiments and more:

1. Understanding that each biome (habitat) has specific flora, fauna, insects, pick a biome and create a chart containing images you've designed of plants, animals, birds, insects and trees of that biome/habitat.

2. Create a historical timeline of the Mdewakanton Native Sioux Indians. What did they each their new Minnesota residents?

3. Make traditional Native foods for your class like Fry Bread and name the herbs and plants the Mdewakanton Sioux ate, bring samples to your class.

4. In the late 1800s when Ellet traveled to the Midwest, Victorian "travel etiquette" was in place. What was it exactly? Did Ellet follow it? How does it compare to now? Make an etiquette chart.

5. What did women of the mid-1800s wear when traveling? Corsets and pantalets, boots with wooden bottoms, what else? Make Pioneer cut-out dolls.

6. How did Minnesotans of the 19th century travel and what form of travel did they use most? Create a diagram.

7. Do a class demonstration using a cardboard model you made of how a daguerreotype worked (camera), researching and explaining the lengthy process.

8. What shoes did Minnesota pioneers wear? Do research into handmade wooden clogs and why there are few samples of shoes from that period.

9. Godey's Lady's Books—Ellet was often published in what could be referred to as a

Women's Home Journal. Two well-preserved books from the 1850s were donated by Vicki Pellar Price to the Eden Prairie Historical Society and can be viewed by appointment at the Eden Prairie City Center Museum. Images are also on the Elizabeth Fries Ellet Interpretive Signs at the Richard T. Anderson Conservation Area. Note that Poe, Emerson, Hawthorne, Longfellow, Stowe, and many other famous writers were also published in Godey's Lady's Books.

10. Create your own journal article reflecting aspects of your life in a story with images.

11. Make a model of a flatboat, keelboat, modes of travel on the Mississippi and Minnesota rivers for tourists, shipping and general travel in the 19th century.

12. Cartography, make a map of a particular area (biome/habitat) you explored, naming trees and plants and their habitat.

13. Bird and Insect Watch: Bring your cell phone and camera and capture images of the insects, birds, or bird nests you see. Create an ongoing diary of visits to present to your class. Let them know what you learned.

14. Rock Hunting in Minnesota, here's where to go: https://www.dnr.state.mn.us/education/geology/digging/rocksmin.html

Did You Know?

On each interpretive sign there is a *Did You Know? section* about each of the six biomes and interesting habitat information such as:

Minnesota River Biome
Fact: The American Bald Eagle is a common sight along the Minnesota River. The majestic birds of prey can fly up to 65 miles per hour and up to 150 or 200 miles per hour in a dive.

Bottomland Forest Biome
Fact: Wood frogs have an incredible ability to survive frozen temperatures, and in spring, warm up and hop away. Land-hibernating frogs overwinter under leaf litter under the snow and often experience sub-zero temperatures. They survive because they have a layer of glucose that keeps them warm.

Sedge Meadow Biome
A healthy Sedge Meadow would include hundreds of plant species, as well as habitat for hundreds or thousands of species of other living things like birds and insects.

Big Woods Biome
Earthworms are not indigenous to forests; they are invasive species that destroy leaf litter where many species find their food. Small species that live on the forest floor are food for larger species, thus earth worms cause a domino effect: depleting the food source for small species, as well as larger animals.

Oak Savanna Biome
Great Crested Flycatchers perform a natural pest control service by consuming more than 50 kinds of beetles, along with wasps, bees, sawflies, mosquitoes, grasshoppers, crickets, katydids, moths, caterpillars, cicadas and other insects.

Prairie Biome
The Deer Mouse that lives in the Prairie has four toes on their front feet and five toes on their back feet.

Settlers Ridge Location
There is also an interpretive sign for Settler's Ridge, where Eden Prairie's first town hall meeting was held in a log school house on May 11, 1858, the same day Minnesota became a state.

Bibliography

Brockman, Wendy, and Marilyn Garber. "Emily Hitchcock Terry (1838-1921), Minnesota's First Botanical Artist." The Botanical Artist, September 1996, Vol. 2, No. 3, pp. 11-12. American Society of Botanical Artists (ASBA).

Ellet, Elizabeth Fries. A Ramble about the Country. Charleston, SC: BiblioLife Reproduction Series, 2009.

Ellet, Elizabeth Fries. Summer Rambles in the West. New York: J.C. Riker, 1852.

Emerson, Ralph Waldo. "Nature." In The Essential Writings of Ralph Waldo Emerson, edited by Brooks Atkinson, 1-50. New York: Random House, 2000.

Estwick, Evans. Evan's Pedestrious Tour of Four Thousand Miles-1818. Carlisle, MA.

Hendrix Jr., James P. "A New Vision of America: Lewis and Clark and the Emergence of the American Imagination." Great Plains Quarterly, Vol. 21, No. 3 (Summer 2001), pp. 211-232. University of Nebraska Press.

John, Gareth E. "Cultural Nationalism, Westward Expansion and the Production of Imperial Landscape: George Catlin's Native American West." Ecumene, Vol. 8, No. 2 (April 2001), pp. 175-203.

Petersen, William J. "Steamboating the Minnesota River." Minnesota Historical Society.

Straker, Robert L. "Thoreau's Journey to Minnesota." The New England Quarterly, September 1941.

"The Botanical Artist." Vol. 2, No. 3 (September 1996), pp. 11-12.

"Ellet Genealogy." Historic Huron. Accessed June 12, 2023. http://www.historichuron.org/lummis-family-and-lummisville/.

"Good Reads Ellet Books." Goodreads. Accessed June 12, 2023. https://www.goodreads.com/author/list/2397712.Elizabeth_Fries_Ellet.

"Legacy: A Journal of American Women Writers." University of Nebraska Press.

Minnesota History, Vol. 34, No. 1 (Spring, 1954), pp. 28-33. Beaumont Newhall. "Minnesota Daguerreotypes."

Patterson, Paneil, ed. Early American Nature Writers: A Biographical Encyclopedia. Accessed June 12, 2023. https://www.nhbs.com/early-american-nature-writers-book#:~:text=Early%20American%20Nature%20Writers%20profiles,Thoreau%2C%20and%20Mabel%20Osgood%20Wright.

"Thoreau in Minnesota." Minneapolis State Atlas. Minnesota Historical Society.

About the Author

Vicki Pellar Price is the director of Writers Rising Up to Defend Place, Natural Habitat, Wetlands (since 2001). The 501 (c) (3) literary nonprofit is based in Eden Prairie. The Elizabeth Fries Ellet Interpretive Trail was a four-year project the non-profit undertook to create a permanent guide to Eden Prairie's history and natural biomes in a 125 acre stretch of untouched prairie, big woods, sedge meadow, oak savanna and bottomland forest. The non-profit has partnered with the Arboretum on writing workshops and readings related to place and natural habitat with Minnesota writers Carol Bly, Bill Holm, Paul Gruchow, Deborah Keenan, Joyce Sutphen and Michael Dennis Browne. Pellar Price has a BFA from California Institute of the Arts (Chouinard Art Institute), and MLA & MFA from Hamline.

Reader's Notes